MW01108432

EFFECTIVE CLASSROOM MANAGEMENT

7 Tricks to Be a Good Teacher. Use an Effective Classroom Discipline. A Cognitive, Behavioral, and Empathic Method to Overcome Anxiety and Discomfort

Written by:

Artur Mc Teachers

TABLE OF CONTENTS

PREMISE

The teaching profession is considered one of the noblest professions. Teachers have great responsibilities and duties to complete in nurturing the soul and mind of the students. Teachers play a prominent role in shaping the future of our country. Teachers are like the guiding souls that provide knowledge and wisdom to us, hence they should be respected and appreciated with all our heart. They must be treated with full respect and politeness. Teachers are our inspirations to be great in the future. Teachers cannot become successful and famous without the assistance of their students. Teachers and students should work as a team for mutual growth and success. Before becoming a teacher, one should have full knowledge and skills on how to educate children with various abilities, personalities, circumstances, status, and well prepared to face challenges in the teaching profession. If teachers are not well trained and prepared, they will be weak and have failures. Teachers who are not professionally competent should be dismissed or transferred to other positions.

A true teacher would be a dedicated and selfless person. They have the willingness to fulfill their responsibilities and duties given by schools in achieving learning outcomes for students. True teachers are always willing to work, study, research hard, and develop new methods of teaching, so they know what strategies are effective in teaching students of different levels, abilities, personalities, circumstances, status, and ethnicities. They also know how to integrate technology learning tools into their teaching methods effectively without sacrificing traditional ways of learning that benefits all the students.

Your responsibilities as a teacher might be sometimes overwhelming. Sometimes, you might feel that you are not worthy of the respect and affection that your students have for you. I can understand how it feels to be treated like that. Some teachers have been very lucky to receive great rewards from their students and co-workers as a recognition of their role in the community, but most times we do not even get an appreciation for what we do.

Sometimes, there are doubts and hesitations in your mind. Are students learning? Are they like what you teach and are happy with it? How much they have learned from you?

The most wonderful feeling is to see students doing well academically and in their lives because of your great efforts. When they get good grades on their exams, when they win in competitions, when they show improvement in their skills, and when they succeed in life. That is one of the best rewards that a teacher could ever get. But sometimes, we do not get it. We just toil endlessly in our profession and hardly get any rewards.

When students misbehave, when they give you a hard time, when they are not motivated and negative in their work, when they refuse to learn and do their homework, it is the hardest part of a teacher's life. To know how to handle this type of student is a great challenge. To encourage them with love is always the best thing that you can do as a teacher. You must never give up on them because life has something good for them and only if you help them to find their way will they succeed in life.

To be an effective teacher, one must be well trained, well prepared, and have a high level of patience. One must have some knowledge on how to handle different types of students with different abilities, personalities, circumstances, status, and unique background. One should always read books related to teaching strategies and educational psychology as well as continually update their skills through offsite seminars or conferences on effective ways of teaching children at all levels.

We should understand that teaching sometimes takes a lot of time, effort, and energy. It is not easy to keep our students interested in what we are teaching them. It is also not easy to motivate and inspire them every single day when they come to school. You have to be prepared for the long haul of your life as a teacher as you will need to stay till the end of your career for students to learn what you wanted them to learn in the first place.

While being a teacher is challenging, it also needs immense patience and understanding. We have a great responsibility as teachers not only in educating our children but also in guiding their lives by helping them achieve their dreams and aspirations. Compassion, love, kindness must guide us while being a compassionate teacher because we are shaping the future of our country by how we teach today's children. There are times that we work hard to pass along what we know to our students but in the end, we see our students working hard and giving their best to achieve success for themselves, for us as teachers, and for the entire nation as well. This is where we feel real satisfaction or joy about what we do.

You might even be wondering whether you are doing the right thing or applying the right method in your teaching. Sometimes you feel that there is a need for you as a teacher to be more innovative and creative in teaching. You might even have doubts if what you are doing is affecting the students positively or negatively.

This book aims to help you as a teacher to become more effective and efficient in your teaching. To make sure that your students are learning and growing in their knowledge, skills, and attitudes. It is my desire to help teachers and other professionals reach the highest level of satisfaction in teaching.

When I started my career as a teacher, I was not good at all because I always try to take shortcuts rather than doing it in the right way. I have learned many things from great teachers with time. Some things were already known to me but I just did not apply them because of ignorance or negligence on my part.

For that reason, I wanted to share with you these stratagems that I learned that will help you become a better teacher. They might not be new but what matters is the intention behind applying them. If you have good intentions, then it will make all the difference.

This book also aims to serve as a guide for teachers who are planning to start their career as well as for mothers who want to teach their children in teaching them to read and write.

One will also be guided with simple strategies about effective ways of creating an atmosphere for learning, helping, and supporting your students with their studies, and also how to make your classroom an inspiring learning place.

In this book, I will also share with your various tips on teaching methods that would help teachers become more respected by their students. I want you to be able to apply these techniques effectively in your classroom so that they can have a positive impact on all the members of the class as well as those who are not present in the class at any given time. You will know how best to teach all types of students with different abilities, personalities, circumstances, status, and unique background. You can use these techniques when you deal with discipline issues, teacher-student conflict resolution, or when you try to motivate students who need some inspiration for them to achieve success in life.

Also, I should say that I have changed or improved these stratagems to suit my teaching style and the students that I teach. These are not ruling that you must follow but principles or guidelines that you can apply in your teaching practice.

By following some of these guidelines, your students will surely benefit from your teaching and experience true success and satisfaction in their learning.

INTRODUCTION

There is no doubt about it, but one of the key things that makes a good teacher is the quality of their lessons. I am sure you can remember back to your own school experience: there are some particular lessons and teachers that stand out because of the good things that happened in them. Today's classroom environment is no different. Your lessons should be inspirational, amusing, enlightening, and most of all enjoyable.

There are many ways to get your content across in learning without boring the kids to death. Here are some ways to ensure the preparation and delivery of your lesson is nothing less than superb.

Preparation

Good lessons are always well thought out and planned in advance. If these lessons go well, then once you have planned them properly, assuming the contents of the subject remains the same, you can deliver this lesson, again and again, year after year. It might take you a bit of hard work and time preparing such good quality work for the first couple of years, but you will reap the rewards for the rest of your teaching time.

Prepare your lessons with a range of activities in mind, and a variety of ways of working.

These might include the following:

Individual Working

You explain a concept or deliver content, and then the children work individually to complete tasks.

Paired Work

Students work in twos to work towards a common goal. This is particularly enjoyable for them, especially if you let them work with their friends, but you need to make sure they are actually working and not just having chitchat!

Group Work

The majority of students enjoy this as they get to interact. Some of the shyer, quieter children may struggle, so it is up to you to decide if you will let them work in a group with friends or if you will decide which students will make up each group.

Written Tasks

Plain and simple, they work in their exercise books or on a worksheet.

Reading Tasks

If they are reading for understanding, the classroom must be quiet to enable them to do this without distractions. Make it clear that it is silent reading time.

Speaking and Listening Tasks

This may involve students feeding back or speaking aloud to the rest of the class in a verbal manner. Did you know that public speaking, also known as glossophobia, is the number 1 fear in the world?

So, by having these sorts of tasks, you are helping the students build confidence by exposure therapy, by getting them to do what they may fear: present in front of their peer group.

Encouragement and praise must be given to all students, as many fear speaking aloud. Do not, under any circumstances mock their efforts when speaking aloud, as it will hurt their self-esteem and damage their confidence. Even if they've only managed to say a couple of words whilst they talk in front of the entire class, for some students this is a really big deal, so give them the credit they deserve.

Interactive Tasks

This may include things like creating a drama, or a video, or an interview, an advert, something creative or visual, or a presentation to present. Give clear guidelines on what is and isn't acceptable, and some students will try and get silly if they are left to their own devices and given too much free reign!

As for having a variety of activities, I'm sure you can remember from your lessons which were the boring and tedious ones. You could typically forecast what would happen in every single lesson since they were that foreseeable: for example, in my French lesson, I could predict that we would go in and turn to page X in a textbook and read a passage and then answer the questions. Boring! Mix things up for the students, so they don't get the chance to get bored and potentially start creating havoc or mischief.

Keep your activities short in small time-dependent chunks, as this helps aid concentration levels. Make it clear how many minutes they have got to do each section, and consider having a clock or timer where they can all see and monitor their progress and time remaining for the task.

Vary what they have to do, and try and have at least 3 different activity styles in 1 lesson. Anywhere where you can encourage them to use all 3 learning styles—visual, auditory, and kinesthetic—will cater to the majority of all children in the class. For instance, you might teach a little bit from the front on the board, read a little passage, have them do a little bit of writing about it, and then get them to do an accompanying relevant talk to illustrate their point.

Any time where the students can get their colored pencils or highlighters out is a bonus in a child's mind! It's up with things like content-based word searches or crosswords—anything a little bit different to the norm they usually see in other lessons.

Delivery

Delivery of the lesson subject and content is also crucial. If you are teaching a subject that bores you silly, it will become seemingly obvious to the students. There is simply no disguising that you hate what you are teaching! So, pick your content wisely, and if it happens to be a topic that you despise (but it's necessary as part of the curriculum), find a more interesting way to deliver it which doesn't bore you to tears, and try your best to remain positive throughout!

If you are enthusiastic about the subject, then the kids will pick up on your interest and also deem it worthwhile in listening to and enjoy. One of my favorite topics involved Shakespeare, traditionally known as quite tedious to some. But by delivering it in certain ways and making it understandable for them to enjoy their stories, they ended up enjoying it as much as I.

Be Passionate About Your Subject

If there's a particular topic that you love, tell them that, because they will pay attention to it more because they want to know why the teacher loves it so much!

Be Engaging with the Way You Project Your Voice and Intonation

There is nothing worse than listening to a teacher who drones on in a boring monotonous voice—even other teachers in the school used to send me to sleep once they started talking!

So if these teachers come across as boring, how can you ever expect the students to show enthusiasm and enjoyment at what is being delivered?

Put Yourself Back in the Child's Mindset

Another key point that always helped me when planning and delivering content was to think the following: How would I have found this interesting when I was their age?

Put yourself back in the child's mindset, and if you think that it would be something that would have bored you silly when you were their age, then change the way you approach and deliver it.

Finally, teaching is one career where it can be beneficial to have a puerile and childish attitude! Thinking like a child can sometimes be very useful when you are a teacher, as it helps you to empathize with what they are going through, and how they would react to things.

CHAPTER 1:

1st Stratagem: Ringing Voice!

Basics, First

When children enter the classroom, they expect the teacher to be an authoritative figure, so you must present yourself as one as well as you can.

This may take some time to master, especially if you are an experienced teacher, young, or sadly, very short in stature! The students simply must take you seriously when they see you, respect you, and learn from you, so it is important that you present yourself well. As harsh as it sounds, students will always find some element of weakness in a teacher and try and take advantage of that. It is nothing personal, just a game of power play, they do the same at home with their parents.

A real mistake that a lot of new teachers make is this: they are desperate to be liked by the students. This is not your job. Your job is to teach, not be their friend. Don't get me wrong, as a teacher it's nice to be liked. But it's much better to be respected.

Being respected means you can get the students to do the things that they need to do to progress. If the student thinks that you are their friend, it blurs the boundaries, and then they become confused if you ever have to tell them off, even angry and feel unjustly hard done by, because you're supposed to be their friend, right? Know the difference between being students thinking you are friendly and approachable, and wanting to be their best friend.

Firstly, you must dress the part. Students don't expect to see a casually dressed down person, because in their minds a teacher "must look like a teacher." This usually means smart tailored clothing, think shirts, suits, jackets. It is almost like a military putting on a uniform, it automatically commands respect because of what you are wearing. For example, suit jackets usually have padded shoulders, which adds to the illusion of strength and power. Of course, the way you dress must correlate with the school's policy as well as your values—you've got to feel comfortable in what you wear, and not feel awkward all day. However, if you look overly relaxed and casual because of what you wear, then that is how you will be treated.

Hair should be smart and tidy, and makeup should be minimal and discreet. Nothing annoys students more than being told they can't do something in the school rules, e.g., wear lots of make-up, if the teacher themselves is doing that. In their brains, it is deemed as double standards and not fair, so there is no need to aggravate their own self-imposed rules by overtly "rubbing their noses in it" by wearing items they are not allowed.

Kids at that age are very judgmental, so if you look like a scruff that doesn't care about themselves, they will treat you exactly that way. They need to be impressed if not a little intimidated by your appearance. This is not about scaring the children until they are terrified to speak, it is simply about exerting your presence as the dominant authority in the classroom. So, you have got to look the part.

Consider smart shirts, blouses, and ties. They look professional and like you mean business, and are not to be messed with.

Finally, the way you hold yourself is very important. You must give out an air of supreme self-confidence, and a calm demeanor. You must know that you are in charge, and this attitude must come across and be exuded in the way that you hold your stance.

You should stand firm with a strong stance, and hold yourself upright properly—no slouching or sagging, as it makes you look weak as a person.

Hold your head and face up high and give excellent eye contact to all the students. You must have a neutral expression, not a scowl, and allow yourself to smile when students are doing things well.

Your Voice

Your voice must be strong and powerful. It is the main weapon you have to use to ascertain your power in the classroom. It must exude confidence and dominance. Your tone must be loud, clear, confident, firm, and constant. When the students hear your voice, it should be enough to make them stop in their tracks with whatever they are doing. Within a few weeks of settling into your class, the students will know your routines and boundaries, and you won't have to use your voice at a raised volume very often.

Importance of Your Voice

Why is your voice important as a teacher? Because it is the main tool you have to communicate with the students.

This is especially important for native English speakers because if your voice is not loud and strong, you will come across as mumbled and ill-spoken.

Students depend on the teacher's voice to help them understand new concepts as well. The second language students (especially those who have been in an English school for a long time) tend to zone out when the teacher speaks. They think they know what they are saying, or they are just bored of hearing that same rehashed information over and over again (I am sure that you know how frustrating it can be when a student keeps asking the same questions over and over about something you already explained in detail once).

Grammar naturally becomes easier for these students when they hear someone speak in a clear, forceful manner, so make sure your voice has power behind it when speaking.

Things to Remember

- When standing facing the class you want to keep your hands free, as this adds movement into your body language which helps keep your students focused on what you are saying.
- You should take your time in speaking, especially if you are a teacher who has a "slow" or "terrible" voice.
- Don't rush through what you are saying. If you do this, students will be distracted and do not hear what is important.
- Looking good on paper may not make up for being an ineffective teacher in the classroom.
- What you need to emphasize is that because of your experience as a teacher, and the calm manner in which you hold yourself, your depth of knowledge, and all of the attention to detail that goes into your teaching—you have excellent communication skills, so can help students understand concepts more easily. So, going out of your way to stand out as being experienced is very important.

How to Develop Your Ringing Voice for Teaching

1. Stand in a large space where there is little to no echo, for example, outside on a field.

2. Speak in your normal voice for about 30 seconds; notice how easy it is to hear yourself and what you sound like as you speak.

3. Stand in front of a mirror and repeat the exercise from step 2 again for another 30 seconds; notice the difference between how easy or difficult it is to listen to your voice and what you sound like as you speak compared to before.

4. Repeat the exercise from step 3 for 1 more minute with several repetitions; notice that with each repetition, it will become harder and harder to overhear yourself accurately as you speak owing to the reverberations in your own body (your throat) interfering with the sounds coming from your mouth.

5. After about 5 repetitions (by now you should be feeling pretty loud) stand away from any reflective surfaces so that there are no reflections (you can have people around you also). Now stand in front of a larger space without any other people around, so that there are only natural reflective surfaces that slowly bounce back the sound waves towards their source—i.e., the place where you are standing.

6. Speak in the normal voice again for 30 seconds, and notice how easy it is to hear your voice and what you sound like as you speak compared to before.

7. Repeat the exercise from step 6 this third time; notice that with each repetition, it will become harder and harder to hear yourself accurately as you speak due to the reverberations inside your own body (your throat) interfering with the sounds coming from your mouth.

8. Finish up by walking around for 20 minutes or more in a room where there are no reflective surfaces; once again, do not make any noise as this will interfere with the way sound is reflected at you from objects in the room. Notice how much easier it is to hear yourself accurately as you speak compared to when walking around barefoot or with socks on in a space where reflections are bouncing back at your face resulting from small items like dust particles reflecting light generated elsewhere in the room—i.e., sandals or socks without laces that can get caught into cracks on a floorboard, carpets underfoot which cause vibrations, etc.

Always, remember that as a teacher your voice is the single most important tool that you have to communicate with your students. By improving your voice and speaking clearly using the techniques and methods in this chapter you will be able to command respect from your students and enlarge your influence during that time of development. Also, by using this information regularly, you will develop a voice that means business. It is very important to not get too excited about it though. It can be tempting to get into a state where you want all of the students to listen to every word out of your mouth, but being able to continue teaching with a clear strong voice should remain at the very top of your agenda.

CHAPTER 2:

2nd Stratagem: Smile and Direct Look

When you are teaching, it is important to smile and directly look at your students. Make sure you always greet them at the beginning of class and even at the end of class. You don't want to leave them feeling like they are not a part of your class. One thing I learned is to always listen to what my students are saying, and try not to lose focus just because you feel like the day is ending. When I started teaching, I would do things like checking my phone, rushing out of there before my students could ask to have any questions, and missing one important thing: teacher professional development. It's important to go where teachers talk about what they actually teach. If it is math or science-based, try going somewhere where math and science teachers share their concerns about their fields. It builds up your confidence as a teacher because you leave there with new ideas for how to learn your field with your students.

Why Does a Teacher Need to Smile?

The students must feel that their teacher is enjoying teaching. When a teacher is smiling, the students will feel comfortable and at ease. They will be encouraged and want to learn more.

When a teacher is smiling when looking at the students, they will be able to observe the expression and facial reactions of each student. This makes teachers able to notice their feelings and their level of understanding of the subject being taught. An example would be when a student's face shows they do not understand what you are saying; then it is your responsibility to help make them understand the subject better by using examples or by asking them questions that can make them think about what they have learned in class more carefully.

What if You Don't Like Your Students?

If you do not like your students, try not to look at them every time possible, especially during class time. Put some inspirational quotes on the board or blackboard before the class takes place.

What Can You Do with Your Smile?

You can also make use of your office and balcony time. During these periods, do not bother to see whatever it is that your students are doing or what they wrote on their notepads. As an alternative, think about something or hear something interesting that has happened in your life.

Your smile will mark the class atmosphere and it will aid students to learn better if you are teaching them. Not looking at them is much better than staring at their faces when they do not understand something you teach them.

Direct Eye Contact While Teaching

Direct eye contact is extremely important in a classroom setting. Direct eye contact shows students that you are staring at them, with interest and attention. You do not want them to feel that you are ignoring their presence or that you just don't care about the subject you are teaching.

Direct eye contact can also show your sincere interest in the subject matter you teach. If you are trying to talk about the subject as if it is interesting, but your eyes wandered off while talking, it will make your students feel like they have wasted their time because they did not pay attention to what you were saying.

How Should I Look at My Students?

When teaching, always look directly at a student when speaking to them. If someone has a question, then call on this student by name and never point or gesture at anyone. Do not look around the room when speaking because it causes people to feel like they're being ignored. This might discourage some students from asking questions and participating in class discussions. Everyone will be interested in knowing what the teacher is saying if they keep looking directly into their eyes while explaining the lesson.

How to Maintain Direct Eye Contact with Your Students?

Be sure to avoid looking down on your hands while you're deciding what to ask next. When you look at your hands, you never clearly see who is speaking, and every student except the one that you are wanting to speak with might think they are not being heard. Next, always look directly at your students when starting classes and ask them questions. Direct eye contact can also show your genuine interest in the subject matter you teach.

Remember, that being their teacher you set the mood and are the leader. So, there's no need to be nervous out in front of the class, just be yourself and you'll be all right!

What to Do If the Students Do Not Like You?

I am sure you have had this experience—you are trying to teach a subject and your students do not like you or listen to what you have to say or may even think that they are better than you.

So, what can we do about this? The first thing I would suggest is that when they are non-responsive, just ignore it. Don't use foul language but don't make a big deal of it either because then it becomes part of their permanent school record. If this does not work, then try talking with them 1 on 1. Ask questions about their lives in general, their favorite subjects, and why they like them, and get to know them by getting them out of their shells. You might find something that makes them appreciate the fact that they have a teacher who cares enough about them to ask for an extra bit of information each day.

What to Do if You Are Boring?

Teaching is a lifelong career and it can be rewarding in so many ways. Teaching is all about learning how to motivate your students, which will make teaching a whole lot easier.

If you feel like you are boring, then there are some steps that you can take to learn how to be more interesting and capture your student's attention. First, try reading some articles by other teachers or books written about teaching methods that will help you become more creative and enhance your teaching techniques. Second, practice these new techniques with your family and friends to see if they seem interested in what you have got to say. Lastly, talk with other teachers who teach the same subject as you do and get their feedback on what they believe could make your lessons more interesting for your students.

Last but Not Least...

Try to have fun while teaching. There is no time like the present and you will enjoy yourself so much more if you try to see your students as human beings and not just numbers in a lesson plan.

CHAPTER 3:

3rd Stratagem: Movement

Gone are the days where teachers simply sit at their table and lecture with no interaction at all with the students. Nowadays, more and more teachers are finding ways to make learning more interactive and fun for their students.

What Movements Should a Teacher Do?

First, you need to ask yourself what kind of movements you should do. You can make your class interested by being energetic and bouncing around on stage a lot. You can also make your class interested by being very calm, but still fun and interactive.

Second, you need to decide what the goal for your movements is. Some teachers want their students to run around, talk with each other, and have fun. Other teachers want their students to listen only and do exactly what they say.

Third, you should decide how you are going to divide your time between movement time and lecture time. Make sure that you keep track of how much time is spent on each topic to make sure that every topic is covered in a decent amount of depth.

Importance of Gestures While Teaching

1.   Gestures can help you to create a connection with students. When you are talking, and you can see everyone's eyes on you,

it is easy to get lost in what you are saying and forget about the students.

2. Gestures are also very important for keeping the student's attention and getting them involved in the lesson.
3. If you point at something in the classroom or on the whiteboard, make sure that everyone can see what it is that you are talking about by using your body language (gestures).
4. Gestures are also important for helping hold class discussions and keeping everyone's attention on what's being discussed while someone is speaking.

How to Use Gestures When Teaching?

There are various ways to use gestures when teaching:

- Whenever a student asks a question, gesture at them and ask them to repeat their question louder for everyone else's benefit (if necessary).
- Whenever a student makes a mistake or says something incorrectly, gesture at them and tell them that they are wrong with an expression of deference such as "Oh no! You were off base! Allow me to explain how I arrived at this answer." (If you are just coaching a student, don't correct them. They will get self-conscious and feel bad, which reduces the motivation to learn.)

You might get some really cute responses from students if you do this often enough to them. I have seen it happen before. The students will be like, "I can't believe they did that!" or they will thank you for the correction and show how grateful they are by looking up at you with their eyes.

How to Appear Interesting?

1. Make sure that students know that you are interesting/amusing as well as knowledgeable when teaching. If you always look bored and tired while teaching, then everyone in the class will start to wonder what's wrong with your life.

2. Smile! Your smile may not look very sincere from time to time, but most people can tell when someone is being fake even if they aren't sure why they feel this way about that person. Smiling also helps your students read your facial expressions and see if there is anything funny going on behind the scenes— whether it's good or bad (or both).

3. Make sure that your physical appearance is interesting as well. Sleeveless shirts, dark glasses, etc. look more interesting than a teacher wearing one of those cheap plastic name badges with the name on it or something. A black sweater that ties around the neck can improve your visual appearance immensely (you'll look much more presentable).

4. Be aware of how students view you while you teach and make sure that whatever you wear or do is not going to make them feel uncomfortable for any reason whatsoever (clothes, hair, etc.). If students feel uncomfortable in any way as a result of what you are wearing, then they will not be able to learn as well as they could if they were comfortable with what was going on in the classroom.

5. Make sure that your physical movements are interesting and fun to see—especially when using gestures during your teaching on class days.

How Much Should You Move, Move Around, or Talk?

1. You should move around enough so that you don't look bored and tired while teaching. You need to remain enthusiastic about your subject matter for motivating the students, but you do not need to dance for your class to find you interesting. Move around instead of standing still whenever possible. Move to the board if necessary when explaining something!

2. Try to move around more than just a little bit when you are talking and using gestures a lot to keep everyone's attention—especially the distracted people who are not looking at what is going on and those who might be looking at each other instead of looking at you (because they are curious).

3. Don't talk for too long without moving around or deprived of pointing at something! If you talk for too long deprived of moving, then it starts becoming boring for students.

4. If no movement/pointing is going on, then there should be lots of talking! If not, then there isn't much going on besides you standing there giving out information that could be better conveyed through writing.

When Movements While Teaching Are Too Much?

1. You should move around the most when you are making a specific point/talking about something that you think is interesting. (Make sure that what you're doing is not overdoing it and that your movements are executed correctly.)

2. Move around a little bit more than the bare minimum while talking so that students don't feel like you are just standing there

giving out information and wanting them to do all of the thinking during your class—this is just as bad as being too lazy to move at all when talking!

3. Don't move too much/overdo things! You don't want to seem like a complete maniac who loves to move around on stage. Your movements should make sense concerning what you are teaching at the time and they should not be distracting in any way whatsoever. They should also help immerse the students in whatever topic is going on at that moment, not distract them from it.

To Use Gestures While Teaching

1. Do gestures when necessary to clarify what you are saying and to help hold an important point that the class needs to remember till the next time, they hear it again. (You can say something like this: "If we don't get this correct, then we won't get it right").

2. Do gestures whenever possible to keep everyone's attention on what is being said (you can say something like "I'm going to use a lot of gestures while I teach so that you can see me doing them and that they will be enough of a distraction for you so that I won't lose your attention").

3. Do gestures when necessary to show the students that you are doing everything for them to learn as much as they possibly can. (You can say something like "I'm going to use a lot of gestures so that I don't lose your attention and I get better at teaching because of it").

4. Do gestures during class discussions to keep everyone's attention on what is being said, but do not overuse them! The whole point of using gestures during class discussions is so the

students will be interested in what is happening, not for the teacher's sake!

Movements of teachers are important especially nowadays with more and more students using cell phones and working on their laptops in class instead of paying attention to what is going on in the classroom. Dynamic teachers who know how to use movements while teaching is much easier for students to remember than boring teachers who never move while teaching. Teaching is performance because you are often in front of the class and moving around. The performance element of teaching is very important to use properly to make sure that you can teach effectively.

CHAPTER 4:

4th Stratagem: Direct Personal Interest (Knowledge)

When you are a new teacher and you do not know your students then the teaching can be difficult; so, understanding is really necessary.

There are activities to use in the classroom to get to know your students; pretty much icebreaker activities for the first day or the first week of school that can work for all ages and all classrooms depending on how you switch up the information that you are having the kids answer or speak about their peers.

Timed Questions

You can do timed questions every single year or when you are introduced to new students. Timed questions are almost like speed dating but in a form of pre-given questions to the student. So, what the kids do is they will sit across from someone in the classroom; you allow them to pick how they first want to sit but then they will always move over one or once. One row will always move over one so that the people that they are facing or having will do the 30-second conversation with changes every single time.

Also, you have to ensure that every single student is saying something to someone different. It is a lot easier to monitor and just slightly less awkward for the student because it does have some structure. So again, these are timed questions and like a speed-dating format you can have questions that would be fun you know, and you do not want questions like "what is your favorite color" because everyone always asks that. What you do is come up with different things to find out people's interests. You can ask questions like "What is your favorite fast-food place and what is your favorite thing to order from there?" You will have a 30-second timer and you can easily walk around to see them talking while the timer goes off, and again they change places.

You can hear some people share out their things and it gets to the point where they are so excited to hear what everyone else is saying and then just like that they open up and it is also fun and playful.

Another question that you can ask is "What is the weirdest thing you have ever seen on the train or public transportation?" Another question is "If you had only one movie to watch for the rest of your life what movie that would be and why?"

So, again every time you ask a different question the kids will move to the seat over which is again organized. In this way, you get to hear either they have things in common or they are like "Oh, my God I cannot believe you like that."

So, you can use this activity every single year and it will never fail you.

Bingo

There are so many resources that you can find online. A lot of the bingo questions are already created for you; you can create your own if would like, but for the sake of time if you want to find one online you can, however creating your own is great because you want to be careful or sometimes the spots are not relevant.

So, you have bingo squares and each spot has something different. Then when you time the students, it is their responsibility to find a student in the class so that they can win bingo, and you can give to winners a prize if you want. A lot of times kids just want to be the first one in anything, but you can give a prize if you want but again it forces them to go around, ask questions, and then they also have to write the person's name down in the bingo.

Now, a lot of teachers do the "drop the ball" activity where everyone plays the game but the students do not get to know or learn anything about each other if you just let them do the activity and there is no recap.

So, what you have to do in the classroom is that you have to go over it and whoever won bingo have to tell them who was this person and then they will say that person's name out loud or that person would raise their hand and say that they are is that person. So, it has to be this engagement of all of the students in the classroom even after the original bingo game is done and played. You have to somehow recap and bring all of the students together to conclude the bingo game.

Questionnaire

Another activity is "student reflections." You can do this with my seniors because they are older, and they can handle it better than freshmen, but you can challenge them as well with this. It is a ten-question questionnaire or reflection. You start with questions like; "What was your greatest accomplishment of last year?" "What was one thing that you wish you can go back and change?" or "What are your expectations for this school for the year?" or "What are your expectations for me as a teacher and this classroom?" So, it is just a list of questions that they answer that you take as the teacher and then you read it and then take the time to comment on every student's paper; if not for every single question that they answered but for every paper; if they had written something interesting or something that you can relate to. You can write comments like "Oh my goodness, me too," "Well that is crazy," or 'Hahaha. So funny" you can conversational and it does not have to be some long-winded sentence but responding in some way, shape, or form to what they wrote. This shows them that you took the time to read their work; this shows them that you took the time to read something that was not graded.

So, set the tone right away and the expectation for you as a teacher. It is the beginning of building a relationship on day 1.

So, these are some of the things to do every single year to get to know your students and for them to get to know you. You can also start that first day with is an intro of "Who I am." Just share a little bit about yourself like, where you graduated from, how long you have been teaching at that school, why you love that particular subject that you are teaching. It is like a small introduction to "Who I am" as the teacher; just before you asked them to write anything about themselves as well.

In this way, you would have already modeled what you want them to do, just like you have already modeled yourself with being vulnerable and so open. So, when you ask the same thing in return, they will be more open because the teacher has already shared those things with them.

So, these are all of the activities that you can use on the first day of school or you when have been given a new class or maybe you are being introduced to new students; to get to know your students and to ensure that they also get to know each other. You can use the activities that you love doing with your students for you to get to know them and for them to get to know each other as well and the more resources; the more information that you give to each other. It is just a lot easier to cherry-pick the ones that well with your personalities.

CHAPTER 5:

5th Stratagem: Show Eye-Catching Images

In my relatively short lifetime on this planet (32 years at the time of writing), I have witnessed a phenomenal change in the way that Information and Communication Technology (ICT) is used in classrooms. As a primary school student, I was lucky to get a chance to play games on an old BBC computer, and that was only if I was a good boy that day! In high school, through the mid-to-late 90's and the early part of this century, I progressed from using old Acorn™ computers in GCSE IT lessons to finally typing in my first keyword search on Google™ when I was 16. At university, my lecturers were forward-thinking enough to embrace ICT by sharing their presentations and learning resources through websites, blogs, and e-mail. Many of my friends in other universities were not lucky enough to experience this.

In my time as a high school teacher of mathematics and science, I have had to constantly learn the "ins and outs" of new ICT systems to help my students to learn the material effectively, and to meet the requirements of senior management and school inspectors! It goes without saying: high school teachers today need to be as pliable as a spring when it comes to utilizing new technology to aid the learning process.

This can be a challenge for many stakeholders in today's schools. On the one hand, school management may welcome the use of ICT in as many lessons as possible, but may not be able to provide the funds to purchase new hardware, software, and training for staff and parents.

From the teacher's point of view, it can be frustrating when one system has been used for a short period, only to be scrapped or replaced with something new. Additionally, the advent of Virtual Learning Environments (VLE's) such as Moodle™, Firefly™, and Edmodo™ has meant that, in the schools that use these, our teaching strategies and approaches have become more transparent than ever before. We can no longer hide behind the classroom door, confident in the knowledge that our lessons aren't being observed. When you use a VLE properly, every teacher in your school can view your resources and can figure out your program of study for each class you teach.

This can be intimidating, especially when those 1 or 2 tech-savvy teachers are doing amazing things with their websites, blogs, and subject pages, and you've got something that seems poor in comparison. However, don't fret! We're going to hit this problem right on the head, and obliterate it for all eternity!

My aims for this part are primarily as follows:

- To get you to think about ways in which you can use technology to enhance your teaching.
- To share with you the many strategies that have worked for me and others when trying to engage students through technology.
- To encourage you to adopt a "growth mindset," along with a genuine interest and excitement for working with ICT systems.
- To show you how to get the students to generate much of the technological outputs that come from learning, bypassing the need for the teacher to "know everything."

I am a realist. I know that the strategies that have worked for me and others will 1 day be out of date. We are on the cusp of a trans-humanist, robotic age where the future would seem to resemble vividly the world portrayed by Philip K. Dick's "The Minority Report." We are all going to have to learn how to use new technology in the future, both personally and for our jobs as teachers. Let's do the sensible thing and welcome this, as opposed to being an old grouch and complaining, like 1 of my former colleagues, by saying "Teachers didn't need to do all of this when I was a student and look at me now!" This mindset is still, unfortunately, rather commonplace. As teachers, we have to realize that education has changed and will keep changing at an ever-increasing pace. Sooner or later we're all going to have to embrace these exciting changes.

The good news is that using ICT in the classroom doesn't need to be difficult, and you don't necessarily need to have done a lot of training or preparation before using a particular system or strategy. If used properly, new technology can relieve the teacher of doing lots of 'mundane' tasks such as marking, printing, and even actual teaching! That's right, ICT systems are slowly replacing the need for teachers to even deliver content to their students! As computers take over our classrooms and learning spaces, teachers are becoming more like facilitators rather than deliverers of knowledge. This is an exciting time to be an educator, and I hope that this part will show you just how much fun it can be to implement technology into your teaching.

Make Good Use of Smartphones and Tablets

I can still remember the first day I owned a mobile phone. I was 16 years old, I'd just finished my GCSE exams, and my parents bought me a classic Philips "brick" phone with a pointy aerial and a cool bleep tone when I received an SMS. I thought it was the coolest thing on Earth. Unfortunately, my teachers were not so enthusiastic about this new technology.

It wasn't long before my teachers were confiscating phones from my peers left, right, and center. This trend continued when I started my career as a teacher in 2006, and it was always a very unpleasant (and confrontational) experience whenever I saw a pupil with a mobile phone in hand and I was duty-bound to confiscate it because of school policy. Now, finally, after a very long wait, teachers are starting to see the benefits of using mobile phones to assist in a wide variety of learning activities.

What follows next is a breakdown of the smartphone activities that I and my colleagues have used to make learning interactive, fun, and meaningful. You may be able to think of more ideas than what's listed here and, by the time this book is published, there will no doubt be a new app or device that can enhance learning in ways that I haven't mentioned here.

General Activities Involving Smartphones and Tablets

Scheduling Homework Through Various Calendars

These will update automatically if the students have a school e-mail address that's linked to a platform such as Microsoft Office 365™ or Google Calendar™. It's worth making sure that all of your students (particularly advanced learners) have their school e-mail system set up on their smartphone or tablet, and that the relevant calendars are switched on. This can have a huge advantage over using a VLE to set homework, as the students will receive a calendar alert on their device when homework is due. Speak to your school's ICT administrator to see if this is possible for your classes.

Producing Graphs for Project-Based Work

Any form of data set can be graphed in various ways by tablets and smartphones.

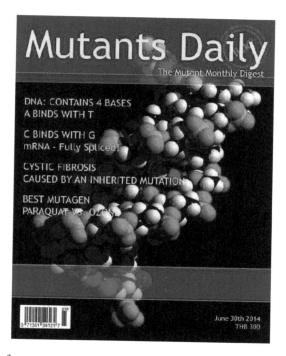

A magazine front cover was created by one of my 12-years old Biology students. You'll notice that some sophisticated short phrases are included, which acted as "memory joggers" when the students in the class used this for revision. Additionally, in the feedback process, this magazine cover gave me lots of prompts I could use to ask the student about the meaning of her work. Very subtly, she had changed a "Daily" title to a "Monthly" subtitle, explaining that this had been caused by a "frameshift mutation"—her exact words. She went on to explain all of the concepts covered by this work, elaborating in quite impressive detail.

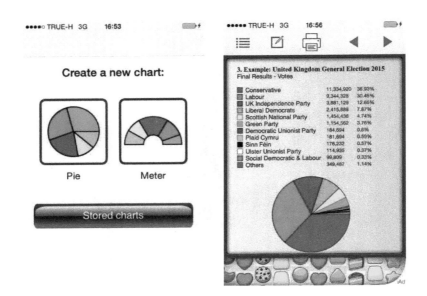

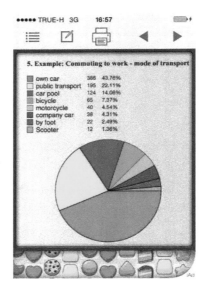

Creating charts and graphs on handhelds can be simple if you use the correct apps. If your school has bookable tablets, then make sure that your ICT administrator installs the apps you want on all of the school's devices.

Clickers

You can convert smartphones into classroom "clickers" that can answer multiple-choice questions. Apps like Response Ware™ (Apple™ and Android™) allow participants to respond to any interactive question using any web-enabled device. Apps like these require limited time to set up, but they can be costly. However, it's worth using some of your school's budget to invest in 'clickable' MCQ software, as it can provide teachers with a very quick snapshot of whole-class understanding, frequently. They can be set so that each participant is anonymous, making the students feel more at ease with submitting a response.

Voice-commanded research

Some students (especially those with special educational needs) do prefer to research voice command rather than by typing on a small screen. Thankfully, modern smartphones automatically have this feature built-in and can provide answers to questions or commands in seconds. This will work with the simple phone microphone, hands-free kit, or Bluetooth™ headset. It's important that the student speaks slowly and clearly, keeping the number of words to a minimum. A good command would be "Tell me the time in Brazil" as opposed to "I would be very grateful if you could please tell me what time it is now in Brazil." One thing to be careful about is whether or not the device is using Siri™ (Apple) or Voice Control. Make sure the phone is configured correctly beforehand by doing a quick test, otherwise you might find the student 'dialing' numbers through voice control unintentionally! If students are using their phones, then they'll probably already know how to do this properly.

Watching Videos

Any kind of project-based work that involves research lends itself very well to videos. Students are now turning to short video clips as a quick and more stimulating alternative to reading through reams of text (much of which may be irrelevant, especially if it's contained in a non-subject/exam board connected website). Whilst YouTube™ is still the most popular video hosting website on the web, there are several good alternatives, including:

Dailymotion: This is a French video-sharing website that allows users to view videos by searching tags, channels, or user-created groups. Students can also upload videos here too if that is part of their project.

Veoh: This is an Internet television service that hosts independent productions, studio-generated content, and other user-produced material. Veoh probably lends itself better to video-sharing as opposed to video viewing, as it allows students to upload videos of any length and embed them on their (or the school's) website, VLE, or blog. Veoh accepts hundreds of different formats and is very user-friendly.

One thing to note about students watching videos—make sure they are wearing earphones and that the volume is not excessive! A class full of students watching videos and listening to the sound through speakers can quickly degenerate into an unpleasant and distracting environment.

CHAPTER 6:

6th Stratagem: To Relive (Evoke) Lived Moments and Emotions

Ask yourself—would you want to sit through 45 minutes (or however long your class periods are) of your class? Do you lecture notes all hour, or do you vary things and keep it interesting? Variety is key. Variety keeps students engaged, and when they are engaged, they cause fewer problems. From my experience, I've noticed that sheer boredom is a major reason why students act out—they have nothing better to do, so why not? For some students, being sassy is more interesting than being bored!

While I wish there were days I could teach without lecturing, sometimes it's just not possible. On days when I do lectures, I make sure to keep the learning as active and engaging as possible. I also try to utilize non-lecture activities as often as I can to keep things more interesting and to break up strings of days with lectures. Here are some of the tools I utilize to keep learning active in my classroom.

Be Ready to Answer!

If you have experienced learning via lecture in the past, which you likely have, you probably know that it's hard to absorb all the information thrown at you. If you are not given the chance to process and work with the information, most of it will not stick.

As I mentioned earlier, there are times where I just cannot get around lecturing in my classes. To break up lectures into manageable chunks, and to force my students to summarize, think about, and work with the information presented, I throw in "Be Ready to Answer!" (BRTA) questions throughout my slideshows.

My BRTA questions (see images) vary from quick recall questions to more difficult application questions. I give the students a few minutes to work with their notes and with each other to answer the questions. Again, this gives the students the chance to process what they just learned, which helps increase engagement (and therefore understanding) throughout the lesson. Here is an example:

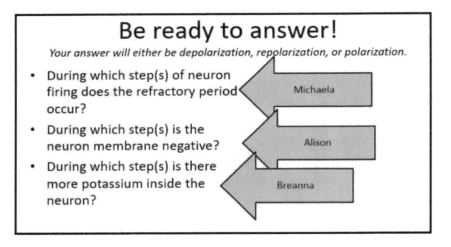

Students know that they need to attempt to answer the questions during the "work time" because I might call on them to provide an answer, and who likes being caught off guard, not paying attention, without an answer to give?

I randomly call on students to provide answers in 1 of 2 ways. The first way takes a bit of preparation before class begins—I choose student names and put them on arrows that are hidden when the slideshow is in "presentation" mode. When I am ready for students to share answers, I simply click, and the arrow with their name animates in and appears (as shown on the previous image). I keep track of who is used to make sure I am randomly rotating through all my students equally. Again, this takes some before-class preparation, but the student's anticipation of possibly seeing their name on the screen and having to answer encourages students to pay more attention and work to understand the information better.

The second way I approach BRTA questions and the format I've used more often because it takes less preparation time is to make popsicle sticks with the student's names on them. I present the BRTA questions in the same way as before, but I randomly choose popsicle sticks to have students answer the questions. When I click on my BRTA slide, the answers to the questions appear with each click (rather than a student name—see the next image). In addition to requiring less preparation time, this version allows students to take notes at home (if they are absent) to immediately check their BRTA answers and gather instant feedback about their answers.

Be ready to answer!

- The sciatic nerve (in your thigh) belongs to which anatomical division of the nervous system?

  Peripheral NS

- Which division of the efferent nervous system would control the gastrocnemius?

  Somatic NS

- If someone experienced damage to their afferent division, how would that affect their efferent division?

  No messages would be brought in for the brain to process, so nothing would be integrated, and therefore the efferent division would not be utilized.

Turn and Talk

If I feel like a lecture is getting long and I do not have a set of BRTA questions thrown in to break up the information (or I just want to change things up), I might utilize a "Turn and Talk" or "Stop and Discuss" activity. I will find a natural place to pause and ask students to turn to their neighbors and take turns summarizing what we just learned in the most recent section(s) of the notes. Sometimes I even tell the students to quiz each other—I'll say something random like, "The person with the longest hair quizzes their partner about the first section, and the person with the shorter hair will ask questions about the second section." These quick "brain breaks," like BRTA questions, allow students to talk about and process information, making passive lectures much more engaging and easier to digest and remember. Here is an example of a simple "Turn and Talk" I use in Anatomy:

TURN AND TALK

- Identify these structures on
  one of your nails
  - Cuticle
  - Free edge
  - Lunula
  - Nail body/plate
- Then turn to the person next
  to you and identify the
  structures on their nail

If you wanted to bring a bit more action to your "Turn and Talk" or "Stop and Discuss" activities, you could have students get up and find a random partner somewhere around the room. I used to do this with my middle school students all the time; I'd say something like, "Find someone with the same color socks as you," or something else random to pair students up. Then, I'd have the students get up, find their partner, and talk about their notes for a couple of minutes before sitting down. Younger students aren't built to sit in chairs all day long, so giving them a chance to get up and move is very helpful. Older students aren't built to sit in chairs all day either, making this tactic quite useful at all grade levels!

Brainstorm Boxes, Thinkspaces, and Summary Boxes

Other ways to break up lectures include "Brainstorm Boxes," "Thinkspaces," and "Summary Boxes." These are just fancy titles that I use to indicate a time to think and break up the notes into smaller segments. I use Brainstorm Boxes towards the beginning of notes to see what students know:

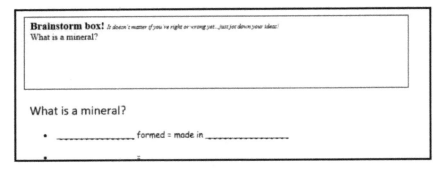

I use "Thinkspaces" to have students take their understanding of a concept a bit farther:

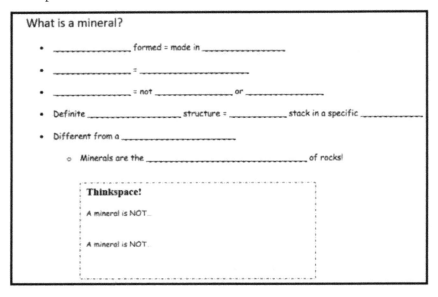

And I use "Summary Boxes" to help students wrap up ideas at the end of a set of notes:

S Answer the following, thinking about what you learned in this video.

a) You have a pond full of goldfish. One has a mutation and has turned brown. Is this an example of evolution? Explain. _____

_____

b) b) A single bacterium infects a person and multiplies rapidly inside their body by mitosis (so all of the bacteria are clones of the original). The person gets sick, goes to the doctor, and takes a course of an antibiotic. The drug kills all but one of the bacteria, which has a mutation that lets it be resistant to the drug (it cannot be killed by the antibiotic). This surviving bacterium copies itself rapidly (mitosis—cloning!) and the person soon comes down with another bout of the illness. When they take a second round of the same antibiotic as before, but their health does not improve—the bacteria are now all resistant and not killed by the antibiotic. Is this an example of evolution? Explain.

_____

_____

_____

_____

c) You have a small garden with dull and bright flowers. You only collect the seeds from the brightest flowers each year to seed your garden in the following year. With each year, you have fewer and fewer dull flowers. After 10 years, you have no dull flowers in your garden. Is this an example of evolution? Explain. _____

_____

_____

Group Work and "Stoplights"

Utilizing group work to promote learning is a great way to keep learning active and different. However, group work can quickly get out of control if you are not taking preventative measures to make sure that groups run smoothly.

When my students complete group work, I let them choose (or sometimes I assign) roles. It might seem a bit childish, but when each person has a job that forces them to participate, do something active, it makes the group run more efficiently and gives students responsibility.

I always have 1 or 2 students serve as a reader to read information aloud to the group (1 student if it's a small group of 3; 2 students alternate in this role in a group of 4), 1 student serves as a reporter, and is the only group member who shares information with me when I ask for answers from the group, and finally, one student serves as the manager/cup keeper and makes sure everyone is on track, keeps an eye on the time, and is in charge of the "stoplight" system. With explicit, active, clearly-defined jobs, I find that group work runs much more smoothly in my classroom as compared to the way I facilitated group work in the past.

The use of the aforementioned "stoplight" system has also been critical a for smooth, less chaotic group work. Stoplights consist of 3 different colored cups, as shown below (if your image is in black and white, the top cap is green, the middle cap is yellow, and the bottom cap is red):

These cups help me quickly get a sense of how students are doing while working in their groups. Each group must keep their stoplight in the middle of their table/desk so it is easy to view from anywhere in the classroom. Then, all I have to do is glance around the room and make note of which color cup is on top. When the green cup is on top, I know that the group is working fine and has no problems. When the yellow cup is on top, they have a question (but they keep working ahead until I can get to their group). When the red cup is on top, they have finished the assigned activity and are ready for me to come over and check their answers.

I admit that I did not create the "stoplight" idea—I heard about it from somewhere else—so kudos to the genius who designed it! It's so easy to see where students are at in their work, and it prevents shouting, raising hands, and chaos!

I found small condiment storage containers (conveniently with green/yellow/red caps!!!) at my local store to serve as my stoplights. You could easily paint blocks or plastic cups with stoplight colors, or get creative in other ways. You could even pose the idea to students and challenge them to brainstorm objects that you could use or build, have the students share their ideas with the class, vote on an idea, and have each group make a set for your class based on the winning design (sort of how I did with the tabletop trash cans). Just like that, you have an engineering lesson, and you also get a nice product as a result. Fantastic!

Colored Index Cards

POGY Cards, as I call them, are a great way for students to quickly review the information and for you to get a quick visual of student understanding. POGY questions can be used as a warm-up, throughout a lecture, or as a summary activity at the end.

POGY Cards serve as the "less technical" version of student response systems. All you need to purchase are neon-colored pink, orange, green, and yellow index cards, laminate them for durability, and create a series of multiple-choice questions for students to answer. Instead of A/B/C/D answers, answer choices are now pink, orange, green, or yellow (P/O/G/Y). I create a slideshow with a series of questions and set some sort of picture or animation to pop up and mark the correct answer at the right time (like the monkey in the picture below):

The type of epithelium found in areas that undergo lots of stretching:

- P: columnar

- O: ciliated

- G: transitional

- Y: pseudostratified

In my classroom, I put up the question and tell students NOT to hold up their answer right away—I tell them that I will ask for answers in about 30 seconds. The reason I do this is that the students need time to think, and if 6 students hold up the yellow card right away, chances are that others will also hold up yellow because it's the popular answer. I tell students that they can hide their answers from others by putting other colored cards behind their answer, or by holding them in front of their body instead of up in the air (many students are afraid of getting the answer wrong and looking "dumb" in front of others). I just need to be able to see each person's final answer choice!

When ready, I ask students to show me their answers; they hold up their cards and I get a quick visual of who gets the information and who doesn't. Also, POGY cards help me see when the same incorrect answer tricks a lot of students simultaneously, giving me the chance to probe for the reason for their confusion. Did I teach the information poorly? Did I word the question wrong? Are students lost, and I need to re-teach? POGY cards can be incredibly valuable tools, and they cost next-to-nothing.

Note that if you have any color-blind students, you can write the letters (P, O, G, Y) on the cards to help them out.

CHAPTER 7:

7th Stratagem: Involvement

Enthusiasm is infectious, typically. But all of the veteran teachers had days when we stepped into the classroom, filled with excitement and ready with a brilliant lesson plan—only to meet with yawns and apathy. Unfortunately, some of us still face a sea of empty faces in class after class and day after day, even though we exude confidence, show strong leadership skills, develop brilliant lesson plans, and schedule interesting activities. Sometimes, no matter what we do, we're struggling to keep our students inspired and engaged.

Generally speaking, reluctant learners fall into 2 different categories:

- Students who care about education but often need external encouragement to get started or keep working.
- Students who do not care about school or who are resistant to authority or unable to obey instructions.

Typically, basic psychology and motivational strategies will get them back on track since the human brain is wired for learning. The brain's emotional control center is alert to the fresh and unusual—especially throughout puberty. But sometimes, what we need to do is change things a little bit to engage the minds of our students. For example, instead of giving a quiz, we can assign students to make a good quiz. That idea isn't really out of the box, but if you haven't done an activity before—or haven't done it for a while—it may be enough to enthuse you. Once students are engaged in an operation, they often appear to remain engaged as long as the tasks and skills involved fall within their zone of proximal growth.

Developing an Atmosphere for Student Involvement

Schools do not need to be institutions where learning ends at the door of the classroom; they can be robust centers of imagination, intellectual participation, and fun. Yes, it's fun! The aim of learning can be to broaden the mind and better understand the world, but the path to it does not have to be straight and narrow—it can be an interactive circle of vibrant and intellectual interactions, where knowledge breaks through doors, windows, walls, and floors, and every day there is something new to discover.

Becoming Teacher Coaches

Teachers who serve as coaches have the same duties as before; they're now taking a more interactive approach to them. Like sports coaches, these teachers mix with others and get interested in everything. They inspire students to achieve results by instructing, directing, and listening to them; they show students how things get difficult, and excitement goes down. The classroom is a playground, the students are a team, and the teacher keeps it together as a coach.

Coaching is concerned with long-term skills growth rather than with immediate fixes or temporary understanding. We describe coaches as those who provide inspiration, guidance, training, and modeling, and who enhance other's ability through encouragement and support. Coaching is multidisciplinary and helps people move towards meaningful action by concentrating on the moment. A coach asks questions that give rise to knowledge, creating a self-discovery climate.

Therapists, on the other hand, frequently look back on the past to help people understand the present; guidance counselors discuss personal issues and can suggest academic or job placement; advisors, who are typically specialists in a particular area, offer strategies and responses to questions; and mentors help individuals to substitute or take on unique new roles.

How are we going to inspire students? First of all, we need to build a relationship of confidence based on a sense of security in a risk-free environment. Students need to feel that they can make new strides in their attempts to ensure the security of this relationship. Second, teachers need to produce assignments that are intellectually demanding but not excessively difficult. The coach's ultimate aim is first to inspire students through activity and guidance then to tap the inspiration intrinsic in students' natural curiosity.

It is a challenge to transition into a classroom atmosphere in which students have more responsibility and choice in their learning. Such a change might make students feel awkward at first, as they are used to the teacher telling them what to do. Since students who take more responsibility for their acts participate more proactively in classroom events, teachers should train students to set their own goals. Accountability comes with responsibility: people are responsible for their decisions and are judged accordingly. As a result, the first step in helping students transition into meaningful action is for the instructor to train students to control what needs to be done.

A certain degree of stress comes with an obligation. Students have to uncover the knowledge themselves, instead of letting the teacher bring it out. Teacher-coaches need to collaborate with student groups to help ensure that their approach to the challenge is manageable. We need to help students explore what is foreign to them. Changing the world can lead to fear of the unknown, which in turn can lead to stress. Gradually developing student accountability and getting an action plan in place will ease students' uncertainties.

As student accountability and choice increase and tension decrease, students should have the ability to develop self-esteem and identity. It's easy to imagine how inspired students would feel when they use a new strategy in their learning, particularly when it's successful. The sense of satisfaction and freedom that students feel after completing their work without being told what to do every step of the way is a reward in itself. Before the teacher knows it, students begin to mature mentally, recognizing that they can make decisions about their learning. Teacher-coaches enable their students to become positive and knowledgeable in the learning environment.

Teacher-coaches should practice reflective response and self-assessment during contextual listening and should concentrate on students' reflective responses. Students are often easy to find out how involved teachers are in their learning. After the students have addressed their group plans in-depth, the teacher-coaches should focus on and reiterate what has been said. This approach is meant for 2 reasons: it demonstrates to students that the coach is really listening to the material and that their actions are being seriously considered, and it clarifies the group's plans for both students and teachers. The reflective answer helps students to either recognize that the instructor understands what they said or, if misinterpreted, to explain what they said. When all parties have acknowledged their shared understanding, the teacher-coach should take care of what has been discussed. Thus, the teacher and the students' connection are chiseled in stone, enabling the teacher to reread it before returning to the community in the future.

Contextual Listening

Mastering the principle of contextual listening takes teachers to a higher level, allowing them to engage in a real discussion with students. Dialog signals mutual respect—it creates an environment in which students believe that their words are important and that they are truly understood. The dialog is not argumentative but egalitarian; coaches and students meet on common ground and participate in an analytical dialogue that improves the work in progress and further enhances the confidence that is so important to the coach-student relationship. The dialog allows freedom of speech and gives rise to understanding and clarification, particularly when questions examine the validity of what has been said. Here, in its simplest form, is the quest for reality, where individuals share their points of view and demonstrate a willingness to be swayed. The teacher-coach who participates in contextual listening and actively engages in conversation is committed to learning at the highest level.

While negotiable contracts can sound better suited to labor disputes than classroom disputes, it is a terrific way for students to be involved in determining the standards on which their grades will be decided. Adaptable to all subject areas and versatile enough to accommodate most forms of learning, negotiable contracts are currently being introduced in a variety of classrooms. At first, teachers might be wary of asking students for feedback into their evaluation, fearing that they might take advantage of it and set very low standards. However, this is rarely the case; students are remarkably responsible and reflective when asked to propose evaluation standards (Stix, 2002). Well qualified students will also decide what they think is necessary to learn in a given unit. Allowing students to help set evaluation standards makes them abler to take accountability for their grades and allows them to do their best to achieve their objectives. Thus, students should not see grades as unfairly given gifts or penalties: if a student earns grades of 86 out of 100 on a project, they will refer to the list of requirements and their respective values to see precisely why 14 points have been deducted. With this understanding, students are better able to criticize both themselves and each other. Once the task has been clearly explained, the instructor-coach should ask students to take the place of the teacher. What criteria do they think that should be used to identify their work? Teachers and students should discuss the objectives before a final agreement is reached that is agreeable to both parties. During the negotiating process, the instructor should clarify what she feels should be included in the evaluation and ensure that no significant field is missed. The guidelines must be made available to everyone, whether in a handout or some conspicuous and accessible position in the classroom, so that students may refer to them as they progress through the study unit.

Building Pairs and Teams

Getting stuck with all the work is a big concern for certain students if teachers allocate pairs or teamwork—a reasonable concern, sadly, since every class has its share of skaters who are on the trip while the majority of the students do the work. I resolve this issue by making sure that I provide some sort of student input in any activity that involves working together. The amount and detail of feedback depend on the students' age and capability, as well as on the difficulty of the assignment. For a short pair share, I might ask for verbal feedback: did you both take part? How would you rate your effort? A scale from 1 to 10? Most students can respond honestly, but even if they don't have their body language and facial expressions, they'll give you the details they've omitted. For very young students, I might ask who did the most work on it, and why? I want students to think about whether students who did not participate as enthusiastically were lazy—or overshadowed by a stronger personality or a partner with a much higher academic ability level. The aim is to get students to find out how to involve shy or less confident students. When the challenges of a group are focused on a single student, there are occasions when the teacher-intestinal coach's feeling is to interfere directly. The best action to take could be to set the student aside for a tailored coaching session in such situations. If a few minutes of discussion is adequate, then nothing more needs to be said; however, often, further clarification is required. The teacher-coach can plan some initial one-on-one conversation with the student before or after school, the study hall, or lunchtime. It is most important that the teacher should not undermine the student's status in the classroom, and that it is even more crucial to build a sense of mutual trust with the student; for these reasons, the student should not be put in an embarrassing position.

CHAPTER 8:

Daily Exercises (Teacher Activities)

When you are a teacher you will need all the tools to inspire, motivate, and change your students. You need to know how your students read and write for academic success.

These are the most commonly used activities, slash strategies, and are the successful ones. They are going to work and if you are doing them from time to time then your students will already know what to expect when you roll out these activities. So, make them a part of the routine even if they are not incorporated into every single lesson.

Some of you may already know these activities and you might think this is nothing new but let us provide a different perspective to using these activities.

Dictation

You can use dictation activities where you start with the text which somebody speaks and then people note down and then they make it into a new text and then they maybe read that out and it's kind of moving language around the room. It is a very holistic technique because it tests all the skills at the same time somebody's speaking; somebody's listening because they are writing and reading what they have written, and they are changing it around.

Quick Writes

You can always use this classroom activity. It is called "Quick Write." You may have always heard of teachers talking about giving students a break or an opportunity to write in class, but do you understand how and what quick writes exactly are.

They are quick moments randomly put into the lesson where you allow students to either reflect on what was just learned or have them just think about a rigorous question. It allows them to process what they want to say by writing it down and then they are much more willing to verbally say it out loud.

Under this quick write section, you can also give your ten-minute instruction then pose a question on the board and when you put the question on the board you can also put things like a little photo of maybe of a pen or pencil on there and that is the signal that they know they have to write the answer in their notebook. You can put a timer on the board for 2 minutes and tell them that you want them to respond to the question.

In the meantime, you can walk around and read what they are writing, and if you see that a student who usually does not participate but has put down a great answer. Because not every student likes to participate as you may notice but it does not mean that they do not have the correct answer or a valid contribution to the classroom. So, when you walk around you can pick 2 or 3 students who usually do not participate on their own and give them the verbal affirmation like; "this is a great answer;" call them on so that they know when they do share; it is adding to the classroom environment and then they would not be as nervous or as scared when they do not think that their answer is correct because you have already given them the confirmation that it is a correct answer.

You can do this activity about 2 times every lesson or so because it is a great way to boost your students and it will only take 2 or 3 minutes.

Think-Pair-Shares

In "Think-Pair-Share," you combine the students to work together to solve a problem or answer a question or some other work. You can use this strategy with your younger students, tenth graders, and seniors but the younger students are more into it than the seniors.

So, in pair share you usually have students link up with a partner. You will give them let us say 30 seconds and when everyone raises their hands; you have to find someone randomly and it cannot be anyone who is already sitting next to the particular student. You put the timer on the board once they find that person and they have to hold hands so that you can visually see who is linked up with who, if there is a student leftover, and if you have a co-teacher then the co-teacher will link up with that extra student, but if not you just put them into a group that already is paired.

So, that there could be 3 because the goal is you want to be able to walk around for the second part of this.

Then, once the students are linked up you tell them to pick one who is going to be A and one is going to be B, and let them decide who will be A and B. Once all is decided you can start.

So, here is an example; you are going to explain about the stock market in 90 seconds and it is your responsibility to explain how the stock market works; use as many vocabulary words that you remember but talk about the process from start to finish. Then you put a time around the board of 90 seconds. Now, for 90 seconds A is responsible for teaching B about the stock market. Meanwhile, you as the educator can walk around and listen to the things that the kids are saying, and you can see them under pressure, wanting to show off their knowledge and you will see there is more information to keep going. You can even encourage them to think back and try to remember the information.

Thus, once the 90 seconds are done then it is B's responsibility to fill in any missing pieces that A forgot, and if A done a perfect job then it is B's responsibility to repeat what A said. So, B is never getting off the hook, and then again for the 90 seconds you go around and you have the students talk about it and you listen until they break and everyone sits back down and then you could have all the group to share out loud what are some things that they discuss when they were talking about the stock market and how does it work and when they did that then you can end the activity.

Exit Ticket

The "exit ticket" is about showing the students their thinking and their learning when they have finished their lesson, project, or something else. You can go from a pair-share activity to an exit ticket.

So, after the think pair activity, you can use the next strategy/activity as the exit ticket. Once all the students have finished discussing then put an exit ticket and that exit ticket would be in 3–5 sentences, describe how the stock market works and you must use words like; shares, stocks, investors, public, companies, and whatever the case may be.

The "exit ticket" is a valuable activity/strategy. The main reason why it is good because usually when you give worksheets or when you give an essay or when you give an assignment it is really hard to grade all of those things the same day; especially, if you have over 80–90 students in a day and to go through all of that in one day and then hand it back is a really difficult thing to do but with an exit ticket you can make a very quick assessment in that day and you also get to know how to revamp your lesson and maybe you need to do a quick review before you continue to the second part of what you wanted to teach.

The "exit tickets" are a very easy way to get a quick assessment of how every single person is doing in the classroom because again not every student participates and not every single one is as vocal of sharing their knowledge, but it does not mean that they do not know.

The "exit ticket" is an easy way to assess student learning. Let us talk about the benefits of the "exit ticket." You have probably heard about exit tickets and you have likely used them before but there are different ways that you can use them and the different benefits that they can have for your students.

Now, on a basic level exit tickets help you do a quick assessment of students thinking at that moment. Exit tickets are a form of formative assessment and formative assessment allows you to monitor student learning as it is happening. So, you are getting information about where students are confused; where they have questions; where concepts are breaking down, and then you can use that information in your future instruction to improve their learning.

A formative assessment which is exit tickets is different than summative assessments. A summative assessment is an evaluation at the end of a unit.

The "exit ticket" is about learning whatever it is you have been learning and about how well did you master the concept and that might inform your future instruction and that is overall not the intention of a summative assessment.

Current Events Worksheets

"Current Events Worksheets" are best for the students because students can mess with the newspapers on their own or now a day going online and finding a news article and then being able to fill out a current events worksheet.

In the worksheet you can use a variety of different things that the students have to look for like: "what is the title, the date, or an idea of the article," "summarize the article," "provide 4 pieces of evidence that add to the main idea of the question that you have about this topic," "is it related to gender equality, politics, and economics?" So, they also have to identify what the topic of it is.

This activity just allows students to become familiar with what is happening in our world today and also to getting the information from a different source that is different from giving a PowerPoint or from having them watch a video and this is another way that they are receiving information and trying to figure out how to filter it through the info.

Political Cartoons

Knowing how to analyze political cartoons is a useful skill for high school students to learn although these cartoons aim to amuse. It is important to remember that they are also biased towards one particular point of view. This bias will normally reflect the editorial viewpoint of the newspaper or magazine in which the cartoon appears.

Cartoonists commonly use 5 techniques to present their point of view. These are labeling, symbolism, exaggeration, analogy, and irony. But not all of these techniques will be used in every cartoon that you view.

Now, to help the students interpret the cartoon's artwork there are 4 things to consider. Those things are the author, the period, caption, and the word, words that are somewhere on the cartoon and are not the author's name.

We also have to consider who, just who the author includes in the characters, who the author is, where the authors are from, all this influences the artwork that they create.

The second component is what. The most major component of what are the symbols and the subject matter. The subject matter will come naturally but the symbols are the most important thing to understand. When students understand these symbols there more likely to understand the cartoons and their needs because they use prior knowledge and relate them to something they already know.

The third is where. Where the author is from and where is the location of the actual cartoon. You got things to consider like; when and what was the time in which the cartoon was created because cartoons are made in retrospect meaning. They are made in the present day, but the issue occurred before. This influences their exposure to the subject. For example, think of a political cartoon referencing slavery and someone is born in 1995 and has no idea what slavery was like; just have inclinations based on history that they have studied.

Lastly, you want to consider why and the most important question for a student to ask himself is what the author's purpose was.

When all this is put all together the students will be able to conclude based on how, who, what, where, when, and why observations. It is a very useful visual aid and it helps the students to organize their thoughts.

Usually, the analysis of the cartoons is a lot easier for the students who have a really difficult time reading and writing or if they are a little bit more comfortable analyzing political cartoons and then you also have students who cannot stand analyzing the cartoons.

CHAPTER 9:

Approach to Lessons

Some various methods and theories can be applied in the teaching profession. Each one has its set of advantages and disadvantages, and must therefore be studied well before it can be used effectively in the modern classroom.

Constructivism

This theory operates on the premise that human beings learn mainly through their experiences. Experiences facilitate the acquisition of meaning, purpose, and connections. These connections are essential to the learning process of any individual.

Before formal schooling, all individuals have a set of mental processes and models through which they view and make sense of the world. Constructivists believe that for students to learn effectively, they must be taught to let go of those beliefs and models. A student who possesses an open mind is bound to be more successful at learning than a student who refuses to see things from a new perspective. Additionally, teachers tend to stay on certain kids because of their behavior. Most, if not all, of these behaviors, are learned in their environment. As teachers, we may need to step back and realize that some of the child's behaviors are not their fault. They are simply doing what they see their parent or guardian do.

This teaching theory emphasizes that true learning involves experience and original ideas that are formed by the student. In turn, these ideas will further equip the student to deal with issues they find relevant and meaningful. Constructivism does not encourage the mere memorization of facts. Instead, it is aimed at showing students the relationship of learning with various experiences that might occur in a real-life setting. In the classroom, these experiences translate to hands-on projects, group activities, and fieldwork.

For example, a science teacher may do this: instead of dictating the different animal phyla to be memorized in a science class, the teacher can opt to provide physical specimens that show the distinguishing traits of one phylum from another. The students must then make their list of observations or characteristics, and be able to differentiate the different phyla at the end of the class.

Student observations must be grounded on what they can see and touch. Applications of past knowledge on the subject of animal phyla will also help them in classifying correctly the specimens. The teacher, in this specific situation, is merely the facilitator of knowledge and refrains from spoon-feeding the students with facts. Instead, the teacher allows the students to discover new facts or concepts and this helps ensure that the students will retain the information and be able to apply it when the time comes.

Behaviorism

The teaching theory of behaviorism is mounted heavily on the experiments of psychologists like B. F. Skinner, and those who have provided evidence to support classical and operant conditioning.

Classical conditioning operates on the premise that human beings respond to certain stimuli with behavioral patterns they have learned through repetition. The most popular example of classical conditioning is Ivan Pavlov's experiment with dogs. In his experiment, Pavlov observed that the majority of the canine species salivate whenever they are presented with food. Pavlov repeated the scenario over and over and deduced that the salivation response was caused by the stimulus of food.

On the other hand, operant conditioning is a simplified punishment-reward learning system. In his experiments with behavior and learning, B. F. Skinner was allegedly able to teach pigeons to dance on cue. The pigeons learned to associate dancing with the acquisition of a reward.

In the modern classroom, behaviorism techniques can still be used to effectively teach a student how to correctly solve problems. The teacher presents a reward—for example, an additional 5 points in the upcoming exam, for the student who can solve the math problem quickly and without any mistakes. On the other hand, the rest of the students who are unable to solve the problem are given a deduction of 5 points in the exam. While this method can be employed to teach rote memorization faster, it does not encourage independent thinking or nurture a passion for learning.

The question is how might a new teacher use behaviorism in the classroom? Why is it important? One of the biggest obstacles in today's classroom is motivating the students to learn. Behaviorism is important for motivating students.

As a new teacher, a great way to use behaviorism is to implement rewards but only on rare occasions and for extraordinary things. For example, if a student can answer a question that no one else can answer, I consider that extraordinary so I would reward them. Another example would be if I see a student stand up for another student. Those types of events are extraordinary and take courage. They should be rewarded; however, students should not be rewarded for simply following the rules.

Most people have heard of Pavlov and his ability to train dogs to salivate based on their expectations of food. It is odd because as dogs desire food; children desire structure. I will go more into structure later, but I want to mention Pavlov's classical conditioning method. The dogs responded to a structured event. The bell rings and the dogs salivate with the expectation of food. Students will do the same. I do not mean students will salivate. What I mean is that students need structure and they will be conditioned to do what is next on the agenda for the day if they are conditioned early and consistently.

I will tell a quick story to give an even better example. I was allowed to listen to a 4th-grade teacher speak about procedures while I was completing some college credit work. The teacher was very strict, and the class time was very organized and very well structured. One day the teacher was sick and called a substitute, but the substitute did not show up. At around 10:30 a.m. the principal called down to the room and received no answer. The principal went down to the classroom to find the students working through the agenda that had been written on the board. The students were under no supervision. This is behaviorism at its finest. The students were conditioned to work through a daily routine. They were conditioned early and often. Eventually, the class had got to where they did not even need the teacher to guide them through their daily routine.

Jean Piaget's Developmental Stages

The Swiss developmental psychologist Jean Piaget proposed that a child's mental faculties progress and increase in capabilities as their age. There are 4 basic developmental stages that any learner must go through to reach their full potential.

For example, a child who is 4 years old is classified under the sensorimotor stage. In this stage, it is unreasonable for the parents or guardian to expect the child to sit up straight and do complex algebra problems. The child's brain is simply unequipped to do that. However, during this stage, the child can be expected to learn how to crawl, walk, and say simple phrases.

In the classroom, the reasonable teacher will not present a 4th-grade student with problems involving fractions and decimals, without first discussing whole numbers and the basic operations. All students must be taken through the proper stages before being expected to perform higher levels of academics.

The Brain-Based Learning Theory

This method of teaching involves engaging all parts of the brain in academic activities for optimum growth and cognition. Teachers who subscribe to this method favor holistic learning to subject-dependent learning.

Curriculums based on this theory must present the students with activities that stimulate movement, logic, emotions, and memory. The problems that the class is expected to solve must be grounded in real-life situations. Contextualizing world issues, or comparing abstract concepts to concrete, day-to-day phenomenon helps the brain connect one experience to another.

One great teaching method is multidisciplinary units. A multidisciplinary unit takes place when a teacher or group of teachers can create projects and assignments that bring in all subject areas. For example, the teacher might give a group of students an Olympic theme and then give small projects and assignments that all deal with Olympic facts and ideas.

The math could deal with converting kilograms to pounds or yards to kilometers. The research and grammar could include writing a paper that chronologically tells the history of the Olympics. The social studies teacher could pair with the English teacher to have students discuss major historical events that occurred at parallel moments in time with different Olympic events. In 2 assignments, the unit has covered 3 disciplines: math, English, and social studies. In the process, multiple disciplines have been touched to hit a variety of student interests.

The Control Theory of Motivation

Unlike the classical and operant conditioning methods, the control theory of motivation proposed by William Glasser states that behavior is not influenced by any outside stimulus. Behavior, thus learning, is made possible by the individual's desires, wants, and needs. An individual will only conform to what is being asked of them if they are motivated enough to perform the task.

Simply put, if students have no love for learning and see their lessons as irrelevant or uninteresting, the teacher cannot expect exemplary performance from them. On the other hand, if the students are consistently motivated to learn more, then the teacher can give them increasingly difficult problems while expecting excellent results.

According to Glasser, there are 2 types of teachers: boss teachers and lead teachers. Boss teachers make their students do their work by enticing them with rewards and threatening them with punishments. These teachers aim to simply have students with high scores. They do not pay enough attention to the level of interest exhibited by the students towards certain topics. These teachers encourage learning for the sake of finishing class hours. Though they may produce high-scoring students, they will rarely mentor life-long learners.

Lead teachers, on the other hand, show their students that every lesson encountered in class can be connected to other experiences outside the classroom. This makes the vital role of academics easier for students to appreciate. These teachers know which students are highly motivated to understand and finish their work. They put in considerable effort towards showing the uninterested students the value of each lesson while presenting passionate learners with more challenging tasks.

Great teaching, in my humble opinion, combines both: the boss teacher and the lead teacher. Some may ask how a boss teacher can be effective. Boss teachers are great for disciplinary purposes. Additionally, as referred to in the above paragraphs, one of the teacher's main roles is to motivate. Some students are motivated by rewards and consequences. On the other hand, some students are self-motivated. More than likely teachers will have a combination of these types of students; therefore, a combination of 2 styles can be highly effective.

These theories are just some of the educational models that have been presented to the academe by prestigious educators, psychologists, and behaviorists. Many other models focus on different approaches to understanding how young minds learn. I like a lot of these ideas because they seem to work for me. As an educator, you will need to find what works for you. It takes time and experience, but you can develop your philosophy before you enter the classroom.

Other theories like the social cognition theory explore the relationship of an individual's culture and belief system. This theory emphasizes the effect of culture on the worldview of an individual. It is important to note that not all theories can be applied to all classrooms, inasmuch not all students benefit from a single learning theory.

To be an effective teacher in today's classroom demands that the educator knows their students by their learning styles and beliefs. Good teachers understand that not all students are the same, and are flexible with their curriculum. Effective teaching occurs when an educator can reach the interests of a variety of students and also motivating the students who may not be motivated by the subject matter.

CONCLUSION

You have reached the end of this book, but do not worry. It does not mean that you should have accomplished or attained already everything about *7 Stratagems (Tricks) of a Good Teacher to Be Heard*.

Remember, that sometimes It is not always possible to achieve everything in the desired times, the important thing is to keep every learning from this book in your mind and never forget that.

You can also propose different moments and activities at the appropriate time, involving now one student, now the other. They will not be disappointed; they will just think that you want to know more about the techniques of teaching.

The exercises will become a good school for the students to challenge and develop their linguistic skills. And that is what you want, no?

Now, is the time that you may start applying every stratagem that you can remember.

And you can also start developing your strategy to teach, which will contain the *7 Stratagems (Tricks) of a Good Teacher to Be Heard*, but in your style.

It is not important if they are aware that you are using these techniques or not. They will never know how much they have been helped to improve their skills, how much they were able to learn, and what a good teacher is!

For them there will just be words and phrases jumping in their heads, coming from your lips and jumping between your fingers when they dictate you for some grammar or phonetic exercises or phonetics dictation.

Teaching has been a long path to learn how to use the techniques of teaching, and also it has been good practice for me in my life, as I could write about it and put some good strategies to get more than before.

The knowledge about *7 Stratagems (Tricks) of a Good Teacher to Be Heard* came from many teachers around the world, from their home training courses I attended or from books that I was able to read.

If you have your strategy of teaching, this book will be an excellent reference for you concerning the techniques of teaching. But if there is not an area in which you want to develop your current skills, then just start with whatever technique that suits you best. Later on, the others will grow naturally as these *7 Stratagems (Tricks) of a Good Teacher to Be Heard* become well understood and applied by all teachers around the world who are aware of their importance in education.

Here are some more practical tips in teaching that I had learned and would like to share with you:

- It is a truth that many teachers believe. They think that they are the only ones who know how to teach. Stay away from such people and their approach!

- In teaching, you should not be afraid of the students, you can trust them more than anything else. They are very intelligent, even if they do not understand every single point of grammar or phonetics, which may be so difficult for you. In most cases, they will pay much attention to what you say and will try everything that they can to understand better the approaches to improve their knowledge and skills and not just "to make it easy."

- Have a strong voice and an open attitude towards the students. Be friendly and they will understand that you are trying to help them no matter the situation that they may be in.

- Never waste their time, if you do not have any clue about anything, tell them and tell them the truth!

- Be active when you teach your students. This is very important because if you are just sitting in your chair writing something on a board or reading from a book or a piece of paper, it means that for some reason you did not know what to do with your students' time! You gave up! They will get disappointed for sure and will never learn anything from your lessons. They will just listen to your explanations to know what exactly does it mean, but at the same time, they will be listening for an opportunity to ask some question so that they can learn more than what they have learned from your explanations.

- Always come prepared for the lessons. Every lesson should be a new journey, a new challenge and everything that you present to your students should be the result of your hard work. In other words, make them know that you know well what you are teaching and do not try to hide any single point from them, especially if there is not enough time for that.

- Do not repeat yourself if you have already explained in another way or said something twice before. You will be boring to your students if they realize that you are repeating things again and again even if they were more than willing to listen to your explanations once more, just to make sure that they understood the content of the lesson.

- Do not accept any challenge from your students, but do not disrespect them either! They are much smarter than we give them credit for!

- Never forget about the benefits of humor! It can help understanding hard concepts and make everybody relax during the time in which you teach them. Just check out some jokes or interesting topics on the Internet before every lesson so that you could prepare a little story or 2 when needed, it will help improve their skills!

Teaching might become tiring, but remember, you are always near to learning something new.

You can even go to other teachers and ask them about their success stories in teaching, or even find out how others have tried different teaching techniques. I had done that many times and I could see that they were interested in sharing their skills with me, especially if I told them about my interest in developing my style in teaching. It is just a matter of showing them that you are a serious teacher and you want to develop your skills.

Just listen attentively every time they speak about something. Tell them what you think about their approach, there is nothing bad in doing so if it has helped better their English skills or helped improve the way they teach.

If one teacher wants to share with you some secrets of their success, do not try to hide your surprise after hearing what they have said. Just show them that you are interested in developing more than before and that you want to become a good teacher.

You can also ask your students how would they like you to teach them. Whether they want to see the lesson on the way that their friends have learned stuff from other teachers or they prefer some other approach in order for them to learn better.

Students will always tell you what they really think about your approach, so just listen carefully! And do not be afraid of making mistakes sometimes, as it is the purpose of the learning process!

Do not forget that there is no single style in teaching, but there are so many styles all over the world, which lead people in different directions where we can find perfection and development at the same time.

It is not a matter of what is included in this book, it is a matter of the strategy that you want to apply and how much time you want to do so.

Remember: You cannot teach theory without practice, it is not a machine.

So, do not be afraid and believe in yourself, you will be able to do it.

CPSIA information can be obtained
at www.ICGtesting.com
Printed in the USA
BVHW051248110421
604337BV00044B/514